SUBSTANCE ABUSE

RELAPSE PREVENTION

A SELF-DISCOVERY WORKBOOK

RUI M. LIMA, MA, MSW, LICSW

2018

©

A Self-Discovery Workbook

DEDICATION

This workbook is dedicated to the people who struggle and lose themselves in the web of addiction, to the people who had the courage, determination, perseverance, and attitude to discover their inner strengths and find their way out of addiction and embraced recovery, and to their families.

The Relapse Prevention Self-discovery workbook is designed as a tool to discover the dynamics of your inner self by exploring your mind and by fostering the process of self-awareness, insight, hope, healing, and transformation. You will challenge your natural feelings, inclinations, temperament, affections, habits, belief system, moral dispositions, risky impulsive behaviors, addictive thoughts and actions, and tedious obsessions and compulsions.

Recovery is possible with the right knowledge, support, and resources. You will remain sober and focus on your recovery. It is your choice.

I have learned that personal awareness and growth leads to an increased sense of identity, personal power, creativity, and greater purpose. The goal of this workbook is to guide you to find your strengths through your own self-discovery from your childhood to the present time, and reveal fundamental components that will assist with your recovery. The challenges of life will be conquered by you. You have the internal power to change to a much better, happier version of yourself. Deep inside of you, you will find the determination and courage to free yourself from emptiness and pain, and you will become your true real self. You will comprehend how circumstances affect behaviors, and how powerful your inner motivations make what you are today. Your ability to learn will change with your efforts to challenge yourself. You will realize that failure is not a permanent condition, but an opportunity to learn, and start over with the experience, knowledge, and lessons learned. You will succeed, and you will permanently recover from addiction. Your perseverance will design your achievements and measure your successes. It is by controlling your mind that you will push yourself to the extremes of your purpose and the great meaning of life. Get up and make your ideas of recovery a reality. Get up and pursue you short-term and long-term goals with intensity and grit. The power of your brain is dormant. Wake it up and stop sabotaging the best of you. Believe, acknowledge your strengths, and move forward with your life.

You are the force that moves you. You are your own rescue. Your courage, hope, patient, awareness, experience, faith, compassion, and determination will assist you in discovering the best of you. You can, and you will recover.

I hold a Masters of Arts degree in Rehabilitation Counseling from Assumption College, and a Master of Social Work degree from Bridgewater State University. I am a Licensed Independent Clinical Social Worker in the states of Massachusetts and Rhode Island. My experience as a psychotherapist includes the use of mindfulness and eclectic psychotherapy to address fluctuations in mood, substance abuse, addictions, and feelings of dissatisfaction with self, with relationships, and with work. I hope this workbook can assist you in comprehending how precious life is without addiction.

Table of Contents

INTRODUCTION TO RELAPSE PREVENTION WORKBOOK

What is relapse prevention?

Relapse prevention is the term used to describe an avenue of identifying unhealthy thoughts, feelings, impulsive high risky behaviors, situations, places, people, and events that may trigger emotional, mental, and physical relapse or damages of recurring. A relapse will certainly cause a person distress and difficulty in functioning. A lapse is a small slip in thought or behavior, which must be recognized, discussed, challenged, and resolved.

You will develop your own relapse prevention strategies, and reinforce your emotional and physical wellbeing by discovering your inner strengths and interpreting the impact of events in your life. You will understand and accept that addiction made your life unmanageable. How you handle challenges and opportunities will pave your future. Your struggle with addiction will conclude with your successful recovery, and your journey through life will be full of healthy choices and avenues.

People suffering from addiction often feel alone. You will discover the person you were, the person you are, and the person you want to be, free from loneliness and addiction. You will discover your deepest thoughts, identify traps, triggers, cravings, and temptations, and structure your belief system. You will discover the best of yourself and recognize your deepest strengths, and what you really want from life. You will realize your full potential as a human being and make a positive difference to yourself and others.

Addiction may be characterized as the primitive way of searching for delusional happiness. We lose our true conscience when we lack awareness, and try to hide traumatic shocking events, abandonment, situations, thoughts, and behaviors. Then, we experience inner conflicts, pain, anxiety, and depression, blocking our full potential as human beings. These conditions will take us away from our truthful path and purpose in life, and falsely integrate ourselves into addictive compulsive behaviors, and obsessions.

The self-defeated and self-destructive thoughts, behaviors, and attitudes are the symptoms of a problem that may determine our future. In order to stop the thoughts and high risky behaviors, we must acknowledge them first as unbeneficial to us and others, and identify the chaos and harm that they had caused. Addiction unquestionably changes the way we think, feel, and behave. We have come a long way into recovery to go back to addiction like we don't have a choice. We must choose to love ourselves and find our way out from addiction. We must choose to increase self-esteem, self-care, self-awareness, self-responsibility, self-accountability, self-honesty, self-determination, self-commitment, self-motivation, self-confidence, self- discipline, self-empowerment, self-reliance, self-worth, and identify and utilize our healthy resources and support system.

This workbook is better used with a psychotherapist or in group.

YOU

People suffer because of addiction. People lose their health, their wealth, their family, relationships, their loved ones, their sense of self, their purpose in life, and even their lives due to addiction. Addiction robs everything away from people. Why are people in so much pain? Why do people self-medicate with addiction? Why do people fill their emptiness with addiction?

Please describe everything you know about yourself from birth until the current time and how addiction interfered with your happiness. Include your interactions with childhood friends, family dynamics, school encounters, romantic relationships, work environment, legal and illegal activities, events that led to trouble with the law, and behaviors that led to a chaotic lifestyle. Additionally, include other experiences and events that *shaped* the person you are today. Please write about who, when, where, why, and how you started using drugs and alcohol. It is important to be honest in your comments, opinions, and observations. Your memory will assist you in understanding the birth of your addiction.

SELF-DISCOVERY

How much do you love and care about yourself? Please circle one.

0	1	2	3	4	5	6	7	8	9	10	+

Do not
Love or Care
$\hfill$ Extremely Love & Care

We must love and care about our True Selves by applying what is known as truly beneficial to our Inner Selves. We must understand and enrich the following:

- **Self-understanding** — (needs, purposes, goals, objectives)
- **Self-care** — (body, mind, emotionally, spirituality)
- **Self-awareness** — (past and present)
- **Self-direction** — (motivation, beneficial way)
- **Self- commitment** — (contract, promise)
- **Self-change** — (courage, determination, ownership)
- **Self- responsibility** — (fairness, justice, morality, integrity)
- **Self-love** — (unconditionally)
- **Self-accountability** — (fearlessness, honesty)
- **Self-flexibility** — (workable; dependable)
- **Self-insight** — (visionary, awake)
- **Self-discovery** — (finding, hope)
- **Self-motivation** — (genuine enthusiasm)
- **Self-discipline** — (control, happiness)
- **Self-empowerment** — (inner force, energy)
- **Self-esteem** — (capability, belief)
- **Self-reliance** — (confidence, thrust)
- **Self-acceptance** — (awareness of strength, happiness)
- **Self-worth** — (value, respect)
- **Self-realization** — (______________________________)
- **Self-healing** — (______________________________)
- **Self-actualization** — (______________________________)

When we focus on our inner selves and our strengths, we grow healthy emotionally. Persistence, perseverance, determination, integrity, honesty, and self-loyalty will measure our commitment to recovery. Sometimes the demands of repetition, failure, death of a friend or a family member, uncontrollable lifestyle, painful experiences, careless thoughts, abusive relationships, and impulsive risky behaviors, lead us to the path of recovery. We must embrace acceptance, responsibility, and self-discipline in order to start understanding the self-destructive aspects of our lives. The chaos of addiction and self-destruction are real. We are the pilots and the commanders of our lives; therefore, no one else is able to acknowledge our needs better than ourselves. We must go through the process of self-discovery, and apply the knowledge that we have learned. We have in us all the tools to be happy. We must remember that nothing changes until something changes. We are our own rescue.

Be the positive energy that connects you to the universe.

In order to remain free of self-destructive thoughts and behaviors, we must discover ourselves and acquire full knowledge about ourselves. We must seek our _guiding manual_ and master our desires. We must understand the roots of our suffering and identify our strengths. We must comprehend, believe, and integrate into our sense of being human, the greater purpose of our lives.

Please check √ what it is most important to you:

√		√		√		√		√	
Relationships		Strength		Culture		Honesty		Creativity	
Universe		Inner self		Reason		Fitness		Media	
Intimacy		Data		Introvert		Health		Travel	
Leisure		Nature		Shy		Appearance		Drugs	
Independence		Education		Trustworthy		Control		Virtue	
Money		Young-self		Acceptance		Religion		Image	
Art		Input		Love		Joy		Sexuality	
Internet		Socialize		Impossible		Risk		Exercise	
Space		Mother		Sincere		Fun		Training	
Awareness		Yearns		Mystical		Play		Motivation	
Growth		Life		Able		Humor		Flexibility	
Rigidity		Openness		Real		Family		Transportation	
Energy		Values		Violence		Friends		Shelter	
Acceptance		Ethics		Experience		Obligations		Food	
Talents		Theories		Lucrative		Work		Hobbies	
Morals		Occult		Office		Sex		Time	
Assurance		Oxygen		Uniqueness		Race		Faith	
Needs		Trust		Sun glasses		Gender		Self-control	
Time		Skills		Today		Things		Alcohol	
People		Softness		Ambition		Places		Clothing	
Nothing		Alone		Goals		Death		Tomorrow	

	√	Please add	√
Responsibility		Other:______________________	
Accountability		Other:______________________	
Self-determination		Other:______________________	
Self-actualization		Other:______________________	
School		Other:______________________	
Partner		Other:______________________	
Strangers		Other:______________________	
Articulateness		Other:______________________	

THE PATH OF ADDICTION IS NOT YOUR DESTINY

The path of addiction and self-destruction is not your destiny. It is not your path. It is a TRAP! Get out of the addictive abysm and find your True Self again.

Acceptance, forgiveness, courage, wisdom, faith, hope, and awareness are some of the many elements that may free you from the prison of addiction. Liberate yourself and enjoy happiness once again. It is YOUR choice. Recovery is the right choice.

1. **<u>Who are you</u>?**

Name: ____ Age: _______________

Gender: _______________ Birth Date: __________________SSN: ______________

Height: _______________ Weight: __________

<u>Ethnic Group:</u>

1. African American/ Black____   2.Azorean____   4. French____ 5.German____

6. Hispanic / Latino____   7.Italian____   8.Native American____   9. Portuguese____

10. Other: _______________________________

<u>Race:</u>

1. American Indian/ Native American____   2. African American/ Black____   3.Asian____

3. White Caucasian____   4.Bi-Racial: ____________________________________

5. Other: ____

<u>Sexual Orientation:</u>

( ) Heterosexual ( ) Bisexual ( ) Homosexual ( ) Transgender   ( ) pan-sexual

( ) Other: ___________________________________

A) What are your Strengths?

____

____

____

____

____

____

____

____

B) What are your Abilities and Skills? (e.g. vocational)

____

____

____

____

____

____

____

____

C) What are your Needs?

____

____

____

____

____

____

____

____

D) What are your Goals? (What would you like to accomplish in one month; three months, six months, one year, two years, and five years).

____

____

____

____

____

____

____

____

____

E) What are the favorite things you like to do in your free time and with whom? (e.g. hobbies, sports, family involvement, etc.).

____

____

____

____

____

____

F) Please write everything you would like to change in your life.

____

____

____

____

____

____

____

____

____

____

G) Please describe all your achievements?

____

____

____

____

____

____

H) Please write everything you have lost due to your addiction.

____

____

____

____

____

____

____

____

____

<u>**ENVIRONMENT**</u>

1. Where do you live?

City: _________________________________   State:__________ Zip: ________________

<u>**Household / Living Arrangements**</u>:

1. House/Apartment__2. Group Home__3. Room/Boarding house__4. Shelter__

5. Other: ____

- How many times have you moved in the last year? ________________

- Do you feel you live in a safe place? YES/NO (Please circle one)

Please explain:

____

____

____

____

- Who lives with you?

____

____

____

____

- In the past year, has your partner, family member, or stranger pushed you, punched you, kicked you, hit you, or threatened to hurt you? YES/NO (Please circle one)

If yes, Who: _____________________________   When: _______________________________

Why: ____

____

____

____

<u>RELATIONSHIP STATUS:</u>

( ) Never married ( ) Single ( ) Married ( ) Separated ( ) Divorced ( ) Widowed

1. How many children do you have? _______With how many partners: _______

2. What are their ages and gender? _______________________________________

3. Where do the children live now?

____

____

4. Who takes care of your children?

____

____

____

5. Did you neglect your children due to addiction? YES/NO. Please explain.

____

____

____

6. Are you currently in a romantic relationship? YES/NO (Please circle one)

Please explain: ____

____

7. Does your partner currently use drugs? YES/NO (Please circle one)

Please explain: ____

____

8. Has your partner used drugs in the past? YES/NO (Please circle one)

Please explain: ____

____

9. How long have you been together?

____

10. What do you do for fun together?

____

____

____

____

11. How did you meet your current partner?

____

____

____

12. What all have you learnt with your partner?

____

____

____

13. How many friends do you have who are currently sober and in recovery? __________

14. How many friends do you have who are currently using illegal drugs? ___________

15. How many friends do you have who have never used illegal drugs? ____________

16. How many friends do you have who use cannabis? ___________________________

17. How many friends do you have who drink alcohol? __________________________

18. How many friends do you have who attend AA/NA self-help groups? ___________

19. What do you think about your friends? Describe your friends.

____

____

____

____

____

____

____

____

20. What did you learn with your friends and family members? Please elaborate the good, the bad, and the ugly that you have experienced and learned from your friends and family members.

____

____

____

____

____

____

____

____

____

____

____

____

____

____

____

____

____

____

21. Were you popular in school or in your neighborhood? YES/NO (Please circle one) Please elaborate.

____

____

____

____

____

____

1. Did either parent have a drug or alcohol problem? YES/NO (Please circle one)
If yes, who? How long was the problem? What do you remember about the problem?
How has this problem affected your life as a child and now as an adult?

____

____

____

____

____

____

____

____

____

____

____

____

____

____

2. Were you raised in part or all of the time by foster parents or relatives? (Other than
your parents) YES/NO. Please explain.

____

____

____

3. How often did your parents/guardians ground you or put you in time out?   Please
elaborate
( ) Frequently   ( ) Often   ( ) Occasionally   ( ) Rarely   ( ) Never

____

____

Please explain

4. Do you feel you were physically abused   YES/NO

____

5. Do you feel you were neglected?   YES/NO

____

6. Do you feel you were hurt in a sexual way?   YES/NO

____

7. Did your parents ever hurt you when they were out of control?   YES/NO

____

EARLY FAMILY

1. Did you live in a two-parent family YES/NO. If yes until when?

____

____

____

If no, why not? ____

____

____

____

2. Do you have siblings? YES/NO. If yes, how many? _______________

Did they live in the same family? YES/NO. If no, why not?

____

____

3. Did your family have ongoing family difficulties? YES/NO. If yes, please
    explain.

____

____

4. Did you have difficulties at school? YES/NO. If yes, please explain.

____

____

5. Did you have behavior problems at school? YES/NO. If yes, please explain.

____

CURRENT FAMILY PROFILE

1. Who lives with you?

____

____

2. How do you describe your relationship with your parents?

____

____

____

____

3. How do you describe your relationship with your partner?

____

____

____

____

____

____

4. How do you describe your relationship with your sibling(s)?

____

____

____

5. How do you describe your relationship with your children?

____

____

____

____

6. With whom do you talk about your problems?

____

____

____

EDUCATION

1. How many years of school have you achieved? ___________

   ( ) High school Diploma ( ) Some College ( ) College degree ( ) Other

2. What is the name of the last school you attended? _____________________

3. Would you like to return to school? YES/NO. Please explain.

____

____

____

4. Did you like school? YES/NO. Please explain.

____

____

5. Do you have any certificates of completion? YES/NO. Please explain.

____

____

EMPLOYMENT

1. Are you employed? YES/NO. If YES, for how long have you been employed?

____

2. What type of employment is it?

____

____

3. Where do you get your financial support?

____

4. Were you in the military? YES/NO. If YES, please explain.

____

LEISURE TIME ACTIVITY

1. What are the favorite things you do during your free time?

____

____

____

____

2. Who do you do it with?

____

____

3. What activities are you involved within the community?

____

____

____

____

____

____

SPIRITUAL LIFE/CHURCH MEMBERSHIP

1. How strong are your family's religious beliefs or practices?
    ( ) Very Strong   ( ) Moderate strong   ( ) Not strong   ( ) No religious

    What religion/Church/temple do you attend?

    ____

    ____

1. Is spirituality important in your life? YES/NO. Please explain.

____

____

____

____

____

FAMILY HISTORY

1. Has any member of your family been treated for PSYCHIATRIC problems? YES/NO. If yes, who?

   ____

   ____

   ____

2. Has any member of your family been treated for MEDICAL problems? YES/NO. If yes, who?

   ____

   ____

   ____

3. Has any member of your family been treated for SUBSTANCE ABUSE problems? YES/NO. If yes, who?

   ____

   ____

   ____

4. Has any member of your family been involved with the legal system? YES/NO. If yes, who?

   ____

   ____

   ____

FAMILY ACTIVITIES

2. What does your family do together for fun?

   ____

   ____

   ____

   ____

   ____

DRINKING / DRUGS / LEGAL

1. What is your drug of choice? _______________________________________
2. How many detoxes have you attended? _______________________________
3. How many times have you overdosed? ________________________________
4. How many times have you had a relapse? _____________________________
5. How long ago was your longest sobriety time? _________ and when? _______
6. How many times have you tried to cut down on drugs and/or alcohol? ______
7. How many times have you attended self-help groups per week? __________
8. How many times have you been on probation? _________________________
9. How many times have you been on parole? ____________________________
10. How many times you had served a sentence or been incarcerated? _________
11. How many times have you been arrested? _____________________________
12. How many sober houses programs have you attended? __________________
13. How many half-way houses programs have you attended? _______________
14. Have you attended any of these programs?
    ( ) Anger management   ( ) Domestic violence ( ) Parenting
    ( ) Substance Abuse Program: ______________________________________
    ( ) Mental Health Program: ____
    ( ) Other: ____

Please explain when and where you completed programs:

____

____

____

____

____

**15. How tired are you of doing the same things, falling for the same or
    similar "traps of addiction" and expecting different results?
    Please circle one.**

0	**1**	**2**	**3**	**4**	**5**	**6**	**7**	**8**	**9**	**10**
Not Tired										**Very Tired**

Please explain: ____

____

____

HELP AND SUPPORT

1. Who can you count on to be dependable when you need help? (Write their
    initials and their relationship to you).
    a) ______________________ b)______________________ c) ______________
    d) ______________________ e) ______________________ f) ______________

    ( ) If no one, explain.

    ____

    ____

2. How satisfied are you with their support?
    ( ) Very satisfied   ( ) Satisfied   ( ) Very dissatisfied   ( ) Dissatisfied
    ( ) No support

3. Who do you feel loves you deeply? (Please write their initials and their
    relationship to you).

    a) ______________________ b) ______________________ c) __________

    ( ) If no one, explain. ____

4. Are you currently involved or receiving services from the following?

    ( ) Department of Children and Family ( ) Probation   ( ) Parole
    ( ) Department of Mental Health   ( ) Rehabilitation
    ( ) Court   ( ) Community Resources

    ( ) Other: ____
    ( ) Other: ____

5. Do you have an AA/NA sponsor?______________________________________
6. Do you have a pet? ____
7. Do you trust anybody? ____
8. Do you pray? ____
9. Do you talk to family members? ____________________________________
10. Do you enjoy friendships? ____
11. Do you feel safe and focus on your recovery in the company of close
    friends? Please explain.

____

____

____

____

CO-OCCURRING CONDITION

People who have substance abuse and mental health disorders have co-occurring disorders. Many substance abusers self-medicate with drugs and alcohol. It is imperative that you take the prescribed medication in order to avoid relapse. Always ask the prescriber about the benefits of the medication prescribed to you, and its side effects. You need to be informed and never misinformed.

1. Have you been diagnosed with a mental health disorder and a substance abuse disorder? YES/NO. Please explain.

____

____

____

____

2. Do you take medication due to a mental health disorder? YES/NO. Please explain.

____

____

____

____

3. Did you use to take medication due to a mental health disorder? YES/NO. Please explain.

____

____

____

____

4. Do you take medication due to a substance abuse disorder? YES/NO. Please explain.

____

____

____

____

5. Does medication help you with your mental health disorder? YES/NO. Please explain.

____

____

____

____

6. Do you agree about taking medication for a mental health disorder? YES/NO. Please explain.

____

____

____

____

7. Do you agree to taking medication for a substance abuse disorder? YES/NO. Please explain.

____

____

____

____

8. How long have you been involved with psychiatric services? Please explain

____

____

____

____

9. In your opinion, what are the pros and cons of taking medications?

____

____

____

____

10. Do you have family members who take medication due to mental illness and/or substance abuse issues? YES/NO. Please explain.

____

____

____

____

11. Have you been diagnosed with any of the following? √

    a) ( )Anxiety b) ( )Depression c) ( )Mood disorder d) ( )PTSD e) ( ) Borderline

    f) ( )Anti-social g) ( )Avoidance h) Schizophrenia i) ( ) Other:

    ____ j) ( )

    Other: ____

What are the most important aspects about YOUR SELF that you were able to identify by answering the previous questions?

WORDS ABOUT FEELINGS

When we feel, we liberate life to its most beautiful human form. Feelings connect us to each other and to the universe. We are able to feel when we allow ourselves to receive the full magic and energy from life. Feelings are not good or bad, they are the amplitude of our needs. We can deeply engage in the process of self-discovery when we clarify our awareness and understanding about why we feel a certain way.

How do you feel today? √

	√		√		√		√		
Awe		Aggravated		Caring		Blessed		Relieved	
Delighted		Disgruntled		Stimulated		Courageous		Inspired	
Playful		Adventurous		Yearning		Disturbed		Tender	
Calm		Contempt		Empathy		Grateful		Angry	
Centered		Cynical		Fascinated		Guilt		Miserable	
Thrusting		Valiant		Useless		Helpless		Overwhelmed	
Excited		Furious		Discouraged		Hesitant		Perplexed	
Accepting		Afraid		Appreciative		Humbled		Dread	
Enthusiastic		Frustrated		Disappointed		Impotent		Puzzled	
Engaged		Irritated		Anxious		Incapable		Detached	
Eager		Disturbed		Anguish		Joy		Helpful	
Relaxed		Daring		Indifferent		Nervous		Passive	
Renewed		Determined		Isolated		Panic		Aggressive	
Free		Grouchy		Grief		Perplexed		Troubled	
Ecstatic		Edgy		Depressed		Powerless		Curious	
Fulfilled		Hostile		Heartbroken		Questioning		Withdrawn	
Happy		Impatient		Hopeless		Rejecting		Uncomfortable	
Invigorated		Irate		Lonely		Reluctant		Embarrassed	
Rejuvenated		Confident		Distant		Remorseful		Intense	
Content		Disdain		Intrigued		Sad		Jealous	
Vibrant		Warm		Lucky		Safe		Detached	
Satisfied		Proud		Resistant		Scared		Insecure	
Radiant		Brave		Aloof		Self-loving		Open	
Amazed		Agitated		Affectionate		Sensitive		Peaceful	
Lively		Moody		Longing		Shocked		Zestful	
Mindful		Outraged		Melancholy		Skeptical		Mischievous	
Refreshed		Capable		Bored		Sorry		Alert	
Motivated		Resentful		Sorrow		Suspicious		Goofy	
Serene		Strong		Uneasy		Terrified		Distant	
Bliss		Bitter		Compassion		Thankful		Tranquil	
Patient		Upset		Unhappy		Ungrounded		Amorous	
Peaceful		Vindictive		Weary		Unsure		Friendly	
Thrilled		Worthy		Ashamed		Worried		Distracted	
Concerned		Annoyed		Surprised		Proud		Loved	

FEELINGS AND THOUGHTS

1. What were the feelings and thoughts that you had **BEFORE** your last relapse? Please explain.

____

____

____

____

2. What were the feelings and thoughts that you had **AFTER** your last relapse? Please explain.

____

____

____

3. What were the feelings and thoughts that you were unable to control and understand **BEFORE** your last relapse? Please explain.

____

____

____

____

4. What were the feelings and thoughts that you were unable to control and understand **AFTER** your last relapse? Please explain.

____

____

____

____

5. What were the feelings and thoughts that made you accept that you have problems due to your addiction? Please explain.

____

____

____

____

____

BEHAVIORS AND ATTITUDES

1. What **ARE** the behaviors and attitudes that **CURRENTLY** hurt you physically? Please explain.

____

____

____

____

2. What **ARE** the behaviors and attitudes that **CURRENTLY** hurt you emotionally? Please explain.

____

____

____

____

3. What **ARE** the behaviors and attitudes that **CURRENTLY** hurt your relationships? Please explain.

____

____

____

____

4. What **ARE** the behaviors and attitudes that **CURRENTLY** affect your work performance? Please explain.

____

____

____

____

5. What **ARE** the behaviors and attitudes that you are **CURRENTLY** unable to control? Please explain.

____

____

____

____

____

____

6. What **ARE** the obsessive-compulsive behaviors that you **CURRENTLY** have? Please explain**.**

____

____

____

7. What **WERE** the behaviors and attitudes that hurt you physically when using? Please explain.

____

____

____

8. What **WERE** the behaviors and attitudes that hurt you emotionally when using? Please explain.

____

____

____

9. What **WERE** the behaviors and attitudes that hurt your relationships when using? Please explain.

____

____

____

____

10. What **WERE** the behaviors and attitudes that affected your work performance when using? Please explain.

____

____

____

____

____

I AM

Who are you? Please complete the following:

I AM ____.

I AM ____.

I AM ____.

I AM ____.

I AM ____.

I AM ____.

I AM ____.

I AM ____.

I AM ____.

I AM ____.

I AM ____.

I AM ____.

I AM ____.

I AM ____.

I AM ____.

I AM ____.

I AM ____.

I AM ____.

I AM ____.

I WANT TO BE ...

Think about what you **WANT TO BE**. Please complete the following:

I WANT TO BE ____.

I WANT TO BE ____.

I WANT TO BE ____.

I WANT TO BE ____.

I WANT TO BE ____.

I WANT TO BE ____.

I WANT TO BE ____.

I WANT TO BE ____.

I WANT TO BE ____.

I WANT TO BE ____.

I WANT TO BE ____.

I WANT TO BE ____.

I WANT TO BE ____.

I WANT TO BE ____.

I WANT TO BE ____.

I WANT TO BE ____.

I WANT TO BE ____.

I WANT TO BE ____.

I WANT TO BE ____.

I WANT TO BE ____.

I WANT TO BE ____.

I WANT TO HAVE...

Think about what you **WANT TO HAVE**. Please complete the following:

I WANT TO HAVE____.

I WANT TO HAVE____.

I WANT TO HAVE____.

I WANT TO HAVE____.

I WANT TO HAVE____.

I WANT TO HAVE____.

I WANT TO HAVE____.

I WANT TO HAVE____.

I WANT TO HAVE____.

I WANT TO HAVE____.

I WANT TO HAVE____.

I WANT TO HAVE____.

I WANT TO HAVE____.

I WANT TO HAVE____.

I WANT TO HAVE____.

I WANT TO HAVE____.

I WANT TO HAVE____.

I WANT TO HAVE____.

I WANT TO HAVE____.

I WANT TO HAVE____.

I NEED TO DO …IN ORDER TO HAVE….

Please complete the following:

I need to do _____________________ **in order to have**_____________________.

I need to do _____________________ **in order to have**_____________________.

I need to do _____________________ **in order to have**_____________________.

I need to do _____________________ **in order to have**_____________________.

I need to do _____________________ **in order to have**_____________________.

I need to do _____________________ **in order to have**_____________________.

I need to do _____________________ **in order to have**_____________________.

I need to do _____________________ **in order to have**_____________________.

I need to do _____________________ **in order to have**_____________________.

I need to do _____________________ **in order to have**_____________________.

I need to do _____________________ **in order to have**_____________________.

I need to do _____________________ **in order to have**_____________________.

I need to do _____________________ **in order to have**_____________________.

I need to do _____________________ **in order to have**_____________________.

I need to do _____________________ **in order to have**_____________________.

I need to do _____________________ **in order to have**_____________________.

I need to do _____________________ **in order to have**_____________________.

I need to do _____________________ **in order to have**_____________________.

I need to do _____________________ **in order to have**_____________________.

I need to do _____________________ **in order to have**_____________________.

I NEED...

Think about what you really **NEED** in your life.

Please complete the following:

I NEED ____.

I NEED ____.

I NEED ____.

I NEED ____.

I NEED ____.

I NEED ____.

I NEED ____.

I NEED ____.

I NEED ____.

I NEED ____.

I NEED ____.

I NEED ____.

I NEED ____.

I NEED ____.

I NEED ____.

I NEED ____.

I NEED ____.

I NEED ____.

I NEED ____.

I CARE ABOUT...

Think about what and who you deeply **CARE ABOUT.**

Please complete the following:

I CARE ABOUT____.

I CARE ABOUT____.

I CARE ABOUT____.

I CARE ABOUT____.

I CARE ABOUT____.

I CARE ABOUT____.

I CARE ABOUT____.

I CARE ABOUT____.

I CARE ABOUT____.

I CARE ABOUT____.

I CARE ABOUT____.

I CARE ABOUT____.

I CARE ABOUT____.

I CARE ABOUT____.

I CARE ABOUT____.

I CARE ABOUT____.

I CARE ABOUT____.

I CARE ABOUT____.

HIGH RISKY SITUATIONS AND ABUSIVE BEHAVIORS

Please write all the high risky situations and abusive behaviors that may lead you to relapse NOW:

1. **PEOPLE** who may enable high risky situations and abusive behaviors.

____

____

____

____

____

____

____

2. **PLACES** that may trigger high risky situations and abusive behaviors.

____

____

____

____

____

____

3. **THINGS** that may trigger high risky situations and abusive behaviors.

____

____

____

____

____

____

____

____

____

____

4. **EVENTS** that may trigger high risky situations and abusive behaviors.

____

____

____

____

____

____

____

____

____

____

5. **THOUGHTS** that may trigger high risky situations and abusive behaviors.

____

____

____

____

____

____

____

____

____

6. **FEELINGS** that may trigger high risky situations and abusive behaviors.

____

____

____

____

____

____

7. **OTHER** elements that may trigger high risky situations and abusive behaviors.

____

____

____

____

____

____

____

____

8. How much cost to maintain your addiction on a daily basis? Please explain.

____

____

____

____

____

9. Are you involved in high risk situations for relapse on a weekly basis? Please circle one.

0	1	2	3	4	5	6	7	8	9	10
Never										Extremely

Please explain your choice: ______________________________

____

____

____

MOTIVATION

The motivation to change comes from inside of us. Everything we do is motivated by something internal or external. Motivation is for human beings what gasoline is for cars. Our desire to change may be influenced by internal understanding and grow by external and environmental factors. We are our true motivators when we honestly seek our True Selves.

1. **How motivated are you to Change? Please circle one.**

0	1	2	3	4	5	6	7	8	9	10

Not
Motivated

100% Motivated

2. Please explain your answer?

____

____

____

____

3. Please write at least three characteristics that you would you like to change about yourself in the next three months?

____

____

____

____

4. What motivates you to remain sober? Please explain.

____

____

____

____

____

____

TAKING INVENTORY

SUBSTANCE ABUSE HISTORY					
Chemical Use History					
Substance	**Age Began**	**Maximum Use {Frequency, Amount, Route of Adm.}**	**Last Use Date**	**Tolerance Status** High/Low	**Withdrawal Symptoms {please list}**	**Personality Change** Yes/No
Benzodiazepines {xanax, valium, ativan, librium, klonopin, etc.}						
Alcohol {ETOH}						
Marijuana {THC}						
Amphetamines, meth.						
Cocaine						
Sedatives {barbiturates, quaaludes, seconal, amytal, etc.}						
Heroin						
Opiates {morphine, methadone, demerol, oxycontin, percocet}						
Hallucinogens {LSD, mescaline, ecstasy, etc.}						
Caffeine {coffee, soda, etc.}						
Nicotine						
Psychotropic Drugs {specify}						
Phencyclidine {PCP, Katamine}						
Inhalants {specify}						
Other OTC Medication{s} {specify}						

<table>
<tr><td colspan="5" align="center">PSYCHIATRIC AND/OR SUBSTANCE ABUSE TREATMENT HISTORY</td></tr>
<tr><td colspan="5" align="center">{Current and Previous}</td></tr>
<tr><td align="center">When</td><td align="center">Where {include whether in/outpatient/crisis care}</td><td align="center">Indicate SA/Psych./ Dual Diagnosis Y/ N</td><td align="center">Reasons/ Symptoms</td><td align="center">Outcome</td></tr>
<tr><td></td><td></td><td></td><td></td><td></td></tr>
<tr><td></td><td></td><td></td><td></td><td></td></tr>
<tr><td></td><td></td><td></td><td></td><td></td></tr>
<tr><td></td><td></td><td></td><td></td><td></td></tr>
<tr><td></td><td></td><td></td><td></td><td></td></tr>
<tr><td></td><td></td><td></td><td></td><td></td></tr>
</table>

1. Why did you **START** using drugs and alcohol? Explain **ALL** your reasons?

____

____

____

____

____

____

____

____

____

____

____

____

____

____

2. **Do you remember the first time you used an illegal drug or alcohol?** Identify the **THOUGHTS, EMOTIONS, EVENTS, PLACES, SITUATIONS,** and **PEOPLE** that triggered you to use drugs or alcohol for the **FIRST TIME.**

Thoughts:

____

____

____

____

Emotions:

____

____

____

____

Events:

____

____

____

____

Places:

____

____

____

____

Situations:

____

____

____

____

<u>*People:*</u>

____

____

____

____

How much did you spend to maintain your addiction on a daily basis? Please explain.

____

____

____

____

____

____

IMPULSIVITY

Impulsive behaviors and attitudes certainly can result in predicaments with ourselves, others, and ultimately generate legal problems.

Do you remember how impulsive you were when you first used drugs or alcohol? Please circle one.

0	1	2	3	4	5	6	7	8	9	10

Not Impulsive

In Control

Extremely Impulsive

Please explain your answer?

____

____

____

____

THOUGHTS, TRAPS, ISSUES, TRIGGERS, CRAVINGS AND DESIRES

Once you have identified the thoughts, traps, issues, triggers, cravings, and desire to fall for or use drugs and alcohol, you are ready to identify healthy alternatives. You must acknowledge feelings and understand how they are part of everything you do.

1. Identify the issues that may drive you to use illegal drugs and alcohol (Check any of the following that may apply): √

☐ Stress	☐ Inferiority feelings	☐ Shyness
☐ Tension	☐ Grief	☐ Inability to make friends
☐ Anger	☐ Panic	☐ Fear of people
☐ Anxiety	☐ Fears and phobias	☐ Bad home conditions
☐ Depression	☐ Obsessions	☐ Inability to have a good time/fun
☐ Boredom	☐ Loneliness	☐ Constant worry about something
☐ Physical pain	☐ Suicidal ideas	☐ Inability to make decisions
☐ Lack of employment	☐ Traumatic experiences	☐ Relationships
☐ Constant sleepiness	☐ Conflict with others	☐ Legal problems
☐ Inability to relax	☐ Probation	☐ Financial problems
☐ Insomnia	☐ Parole	☐ Gambling
☐ Recurrent dreams	☐ Homeless	☐ Job problems
☐ Nightmares	☐ Sexual orientation	☐ Inability to keep a job
☐ Hallucinations	☐ Sexual problems	☐ Family problems
☐ Mood swings	☐ Medical problems	☐ Other:__________
☐ Peer pressure: ___	☐ Unemployment:__________	☐ Other:__________

Other (Specify):

____

____

____

2. Please explain in detail how the issues you have checked √ may drive you to use drugs and/or drink alcohol.

____

____

____

____

____

____

____

PLANNING ACTIVITIES

Stress is one of the major reasons why people try to escape from their reality by using drugs and alcohol.

1. Please check √the activities that you think will be most helpful to assist you in reducing your daily stress.

☐ Meditating	☐ Praying	☐ Laughing
☐ Journaling	☐ Attending church	☐ Partying
☐ Finding hobbies	☐ Attending bible study	☐ Playing sports
☐ Attending self-help meetings	☐ Listening to music	☐ Spending time with family
☐ Attending AA meetings	☐ Reading a book, magazine	☐ Playing video games
☐ Attending NA meetings	☐ Watching TV	☐ Helping others
☐ Attending GA meetings	☐ Going to the park	☐ Eating your favorite food
☐ Going to the gym	☐ Going to the movies	☐ Treating yourself with new stuff
☐ Exercising with a friend	☐ Gardening	☐ Increasing romance
☐ Exercising alone	☐ Cleaning	☐ Dating
☐ Walking	☐ Washing	☐ Taking my partner out to dinner
☐ Talking to a friend	☐ Doing house chores	☐ Practicing mindfulness
☐ Talking to a family member	☐ Going for a ride	☐ Practicing Yoga
☐ Talking to your sponsor	☐ Shopping	☐ Other:__________
☐ Talking to your counselor	☐ Attending school	☐ Other:__________

2. Please explain in detail how the activities you checked √will assist you to reduce stress and remain **FOCUSED** on your recovery.

____

____

____

____

____

____

____

____

____

____

____

____

____

CHANGE AND RECOVERY

In recovery, change is only achieved by increasing personal accountability and responsibility. We motivate ourselves by improving insight into our self-defeated, self-destructive attitudes and behaviors, and by genuinely retaining awareness of what we really want from life.

Are you determined to change your life for the better? Do you want to remain sober and focus on your recovery? Can you motivate, educate, and empower yourself to remain focused on your recovery? Are you ready to change your lifestyle and generate healthy habits? Are you confident and honest about your recovery?

Can you? YES/NO Will you? YES/NO

1. Think about your **LAST RELAPSE** and write why you relapsed? What happened?

____

____

____

____

____

2. What could you have **DONE** differently?

____

____

____

____

____

3. Why did you **REALLY** relapse?

____

____

____

____

4. How many times in the **PAST** did you promise not to use drugs or alcohol? Please explain.

____

____

____

5. What is going to be different **NOW**? Why do you want to remain sober **NOW**?

____

____

____

____

6. Do you think that since you **DECIDED** to **CHANGE** and focus on your
    recovery, you have been feeling frustrated, irritated, angry and impatient?
    YES/NO. Please explain.

____

____

____

____

7. Identify seven **SITUATIONS** you must avoid in order to remain free of
    temptations, triggers, cravings, thoughts of using, and ultimately relapse.

    1. ____

    2. ____

    3. ____

    4. ____

    5. ____

    6. ____

    7. ____

8. Identify the name of three **PEOPLE** you must avoid in order to remain free of
    temptations, triggers, cravings, thoughts of using, and ultimately relapse.

1.____

2.____

3.____

9. Identify three **PLACES** you must avoid in order to remain focused on your recovery.

1.____

2.____

3.____

10. Identify three **DECISIONS** you must **MAKE DAILY** in order to remain free of temptations, triggers, cravings, thoughts of using, and ultimately relapse.

1.____

2.____

3.____

11. Identify three **HIGH RISK BEHAVIORS** you must avoid in order to escape temptations, triggers, cravings, and thoughts to use drugs and/or alcohol.

1.____

2.____

3.____

12. Identify the name of three **PEOPLE** you can reach when you feel temptations, triggers, cravings, and thoughts to use drugs and/or alcohol.

1.____

2.____

3.____

13. Identify three **HEALTHY** coping skills that you must use when you feel temptations, triggers, cravings, and thoughts to use drugs and/or alcohol.

1.____

2.____

3.____

14. Identify two **UNHEALTHY** coping skills that you must **AVOID** when you feel
temptations, triggers, cravings, and thoughts to use drugs and/or alcohol.

1.____

2.____

15. Identify the name of three **PEOPLE** you can reach when you feel temptations,
triggers, cravings, and thoughts to use drugs and/or alcohol.

1.____

2.____

3.____

16. Identify three **PHYSICAL** signs of **STRESS** that may affect your recovery.
Please explain. (e.g. headaches, sleep disruption, loss of appetite)

1.____

2.____

3.____

17. Identify three **EMOTIONAL** signs of **STRESS** that may affect your recovery.
Please explain. (e.g. sadness, anxiety, excessive worrying))

1.____

2.____

3.____

18. Identify three **MENTAL** signs of **STRESS** that may affect your recovery.
Please explain. (e.g. lack of confidence, poor concentration, forgetfulness)

1.____

2.____

3.____

LIFESTYLE

A lifestyle is a way of living and a way of life with certain habits, attitudes, morals, principles, economic status, and other aspects that may shape an individual or a group. We may have a unique lifestyle with similar aspects. Sometimes a person needs to change everything in order to remain sober and focus on recovery. The changes may include employment, friendships, location, environment, diet, belief system, partnerships, relationships, and other aspects that have direct and indirect roots into addiction.

If your lifestyle includes the *'culture of drugs and alcohol'*, you must change your lifestyle in order to continue focus on your recovery. If you don't change your lifestyle you are will be deceiving your own beliefs, and allowing denial and delusional thoughts to enter your recovery.

1. **How motivated are you to change your LIFESTYLE? Please circle one.**

0	1	2	3	4	5	6	7	8	9	10

Not
Motivated
                                             100% Motivated

2. What do you **NEED** to change about your lifestyle?

____

____

____

3. What do you **WANT** to change about your lifestyle?

____

____

____

4. What **WOULD** you change about your lifestyle?

____

____

____

5. What **CAN** you change about your lifestyle?

____

____

____

STRESS AND WARNING SIGNS

A person is usually sober before relapsing. The decision to relapse is made when the person is clear-headed or sober. The justification to use drugs and alcohol again may be due to emotional, physical, environmental, and social factors. We change our normal way of living due to the demands of stress, and may feel physically, emotionally, mentally, and spiritually overwhelmed.

1. When you are stressed, your mind is ________________________________

0	1	2	3	4	5	6	7	8	9	10

Clear Mind

Trouble Thinking Clear

Before your last relapse:

Please circle one

a)	Did you think about the same over and over?	YES/NO
b)	Did you dream about using drugs?	YES/NO
c)	Did you have mood swings?	YES/NO
d)	Did you have trouble remembering things?	YES/NO
e)	Did you have trouble managing daily stress?	YES/NO
f)	Did you feel shame and guilt?	YES/NO
g)	Did you feel easily frustrated and irritated?	YES/NO
h)	Did you feel hopeless, anxious, and depressed?	YES/NO
i)	Did you think about the friends who you use drugs with?	YES/NO
j)	Did you think about the places where you used drugs?	YES/NO
k)	Did you think about easy ways to make money?	YES/NO
l)	Did you feel bored?	YES/NO
m)	Did you feel that you didn't care much about anything?	YES/NO
n)	Did you feel sorrow about your life?	YES/NO
o)	Did you feel that you were alone?	YES/NO
p)	Did you feel that you didn't have any alternatives but to use drugs?	YES/NO
q)	Did you feel you were running out of time to better yourself?	YES/NO
r)	Did you stop attending self-help group meetings? (e.g. NA, AA)	YES/NO
s)	Did you replace one substance with other? (e.g. stopped using heroin but drank alcohol or gambled)	YES/NO
t)	Did you feel that you had social pressure to use drugs?	YES/NO
u)	Did you feel that you didn't deserve to be clean?	YES/NO
v)	Did you feel that you needed to have more fun?	YES/NO
w)	Were exposed to objects of addiction? (e.g. syringe, smells)	YES/NO
x)	Did you visit locations and friends who use drugs?	YES/NO
y)	Did you neglect healthy habits?	YES/NO
z)	Did you go back to the same habits and lifestyle?	YES/NO

2.) How many questions have you answered: YES____________ NO____________
Reflect and explain your answers.

____

____

____

____

____

____

____

____

____

____

3. How do you react to stress?

Physically: (e.g. Lack of energy, sleep disturbances)

____

____

____

____

Emotionally/Mentally: (e.g. irritability, nervousness, edginess)

____

____

____

____

Behaviorally: (e.g. angry outbursts, less sleep)

____

____

____

____

____

____

4. Identify your daily, weekly, monthly, yearly stressors.

Daily:

____

____

____

____

Explain: ____

____

____

____

____

Weekly:

____

____

____

____

Explain: ____

____

____

____

____

Monthly:

____

____

____

____

Explain: ____

____

____

____

Yearly:

____

____

____

____

Explain: ____

____

____

____

5. How can you **MANAGE** stress? Please identify at least seven ways you can manage and reduce stress. (e.g. plan your time, prioritize, organize, exercise, speak with a friend, apply relaxation and meditation techniques)

1.____

2.____

3.____

4.____

5.____

6.____

7.____

LIES, FEARS AND MANIPULATION

Addiction may bring to our lifestyle lies, fears, manipulation, and deception. We lie because we still use drugs or drink alcohol. We manipulate to get what we want. We lie because we fear the truth, and deception is the only way we know to overcome it. Our lies grow as much as our addiction, and ultimately, we find ourselves lying only to ourselves. We lie, manipulate, and fear, because we are in denial about our chaotic lives dominated by addiction. We manipulate because we falsely perceive our immediate needs. We do not regain control by lying or manipulating. It is an illusion. We find ourselves inside of a vicious cycle of lies, fears, manipulation, and deception, chasing the subject of addiction.

1. Write seven **LIES** you use when under the influence of drugs or alcohol.

    1.____

    2.____

    3.____

    4.____

    5.____

    6.____

    7.____

2. Why did you lie? Write about some situations where you lied.

    ____

    ____

    ____

    ____

    ____

3. Why did you manipulate? Write some events where you used manipulation.

    ____

    ____

    ____

    ____

    ____

4. Besides lying and manipulating did you behave aggressively to get want you wanted? YES/NO. Please elaborate.

____

____

____

____

5. NOW--How difficult is for you to remain honest? **(No lies or manipulation)**

0	1	2	3	4	5	6	7	8	9	10

Not Difficult   **Very Difficult**

6. How many fears do you have?

0	1	2	3	4	5	6	7	8	9	10 +

7. Please elaborate about your fears.

____

____

____

____

8. What do you fear the most?

____

____

____

____

9. Please describe your plan to conquer your fears.

____

____

____

____

ANGER AND ADDICTION

Anger is a strong emotion. We have all got hurt at least one time and felt angry about something or someone. How do we cope with anger? How do we manage frustration, provocation, irritation, disappointment, stress, conflict, and resentment? How do we identify physical, emotional and cognitive cues that may trigger these feelings?

Uncontrollable anger can lead to legal problems. We must recognize what causes or triggers anger, and deal with emotional and physical pain without drugs or alcohol. We must identify what is hurting inside of us in a therapeutic environment, and learn to forgive and heal. We must enhance consciousness of angry feelings by nourishing acceptance and recognizing the advantages of forgiving past hurtful situations. We must forgive ourselves and move forward.

How can we deal with anger without numbing it with drugs or alcohol?

We must improve our inner and interpersonal relationships, and maintain a positive attitude. We must learn anger management coping skills by increasing a comprehension of our body, mind, and emotion patterns. We must learn to apply healthy communication skills, assertiveness, conflict resolution, decision making, problem solving, mindfulness, and permanently establish control over impulsive thoughts and behaviors.

1. When you are angry do you use drugs or alcohol? YES/NO. Please explain.

____

____

____

____

2. Do you feel angry after using drugs and alcohol? YES/NO. Please explain.

____

____

____

____

3. How do you manage your anger?

____

____

____

____

4. How do you know when you are angry? What happens to you physically, mentally, emotionally?

____

____

____

____

Please indicate √ your symptoms of anger.

Physical Signs	**Mental Signs**	**Emotional Signs**	**Behavior**
Rapid heart beat	Rage	Racing thoughts	Running
Stomach ache	Aggressive thoughts	Overwhelmed	Violent
Sweating palms	Irritation	Anxious	Pacing
Tense Muscles	Confusion	Sad	Yelling
Tight Chest	Shutdown	Depressed	Spiting
Hot neck/ face	Disorganized thoughts	Nervous	Swearing
Clenching jaws	Guilt	Harmful thoughts	Throwing
Clenching teeth	Shame	Other:__________	Laughing
Dizziness	Lack of concentration	Other:__________	Passive
Tingling	Fantasies	Other:__________	Aggressive
Tight chest	Mood change		Assertive
Shaking	Other:______________		Indifferent
Headache	Other:______________		Other:________
Fatigue			Other:________
Other:______________			

5. How difficult is it for you to maintain self-control after having the above symptoms?

0	**1**	**2**	**3**	**4**	**5**	**6**	**7**	**8**	**9**	**10**
Not Difficult										**Very Difficult**

Please explain:

____

____

6. List the first signs you have noticed about when you start getting angry (Physical, emotional, mental behavior, other).

____

____

____

____

____

7. What makes you angry?

____

____

____

____

____

8. What does not make you angry?

____

____

____

____

____

____

9. How do you react when you are angry? Please describe at least three past situations and how you reacted then.

____

____

____

____

____

10. Did you have legal issues because of your uncontrollable anger? YES/NO. Please describe past and present events.

____

____

____

____

____

11. What negative behaviors would you like to avoid when you have uncontrollable anger?

____

____

____

____

12. What is your plan to control your anger?

____

____

____

____

13. Identify seven positive reactions that you may practice to control your anger. (e.g. walk away, exercise)

1.____

2.____

3.____

4.____

5.____

6.____

7.____

14. Please list below the people affected by your anger, and the things, places and other stuff damaged or destroyed because of your anger.

	People (e.g. partner)	Things (e.g. T.V.)	Places (e.g. apartment)	Other (e.g. freedom)
1.				
2.				
3.				
4.				
5.				
6.				
7.				
8.				
9.				
10.				
11.				
12.				

Please reflect, elaborate, and discuss about what you wrote above.

____

____

____

____

____

____

____

____

____

____

____

____

CONFLICTS AND CHOICES

Addiction can produce inner conflicts and conflict between people. We must investigate the roots of a conflict and understand that it arises from many individual differences. We must be aware of our needs, and figure out why we are truly in conflict with ourselves and others. Conflict encourages us to examine issues wisely and inspire solutions. The turmoil of our values, perceptions, desires, ideas, morals, beliefs, attitudes and, tendencies are what give way to conflict. When in conflict with others, we must be mindful of our emotions and behaviors, and try to comprehend the emotions and behaviors of others, in a calm, relaxed, consistent, fair and alert way. We must pay attention to nonverbal communication and entertain win/win resolutions.

1. Have you relapsed because of a conflict with a person? (e.g. your partner) YES/NO. Please explain.

____

____

____

____

____

____

2. Have you relapsed because of conflict with your inner self? (e.g. daily contradictions, struggle with decisions) YES/NO. Please explain.

____

____

____

____

____

____

3. Do you feel uncomfortable, stressed, or agitated when you are in conflict with yourself or others? YES/NO. Please explain.

____

____

____

____

____

____

4. Are you able to think about positive outcomes when in conflict with others?
    YES/NO. Please explain.

____

____

____

____

____

____

5. How do you resolve a conflict with somebody? Do you effectively listen? Do you
    reflect about what is being said or done to resolve the conflict? Please explain
    how you have resolved a personal conflict?

____

____

____

____

____

____

____

____

____

____

6. When in conflict with others, do you clarify, acknowledge, discuss, and establish
    common goals that are beneficial to both parties? YES/NO. Please illustrate by
    explaining a conflict you have had in the past.

____

____

____

____

____

____

7. Are you able to identify barriers to resolve a conflict, and in a positive, calm way agree to the best way to resolve the conflict? YES/NO. Please illustrate by explaining a conflict you have had.

____

____

____

____

____

____

8. Would you take responsibility and accountability for a conflict? YES/NO. Please illustrate by explaining a conflict that had a resolution.

____

____

____

____

____

____

1. **How capable are you in finding a RESOLUTION for a conflict without breaking the law or using drugs?**

Please circle one

0	1	2	3	4	5	6	7	8	9	10
Not capable										Extremely capable

Please explain your answer:

____

____

____

____

RELATIONSHIPS

Relationships are necessary in our society. Healthy relationships have a great impact in the prevention of relapse. We may or may not have a healthy relationship with ourselves, our family, with our co-workers, or a romantic relationship. Our perceptions about our healthy or unhealthy relationships may vary with our belief system and the level of acceptance or denial. Unhealthy relationships sometimes deliver enough force of shame, guilt, frustration, pain, resentment, and annoyance to give up recovery and entertain relapse. A healthy connection between two people must be based on mutual respect, trust, loyalty, good communication, honesty, and a sense of own identity and care.

1. In your opinion, what makes a healthy relationship? (e.g. mutual respect)

____

____

____

____

2. In your opinion, what makes an unhealthy relationship? (e.g. attempt to control or manipulate others)

____

____

____

____

3. What makes a healthy romantic relationship? Please check √ what you agree.

Write other

☐ Fairness	☐ Support	☐ Ability to express	☐ _______
☐ Love	☐ Consistency	☐ No violence	☐ _______
☐ Arguments	☐ Good communication	☐ Feeling of safety	☐ _______
☐ Mental stress	☐ Sincerity	☐ No fear	☐ _______
☐ Instigation	☐ Honesty	☐ Appreciation	☐ _______
☐ Nagging	☐ Mutual respect	☐ Care	☐ _______
☐ Gossip	☐ Humor	☐ Connection	☐ _______
☐ Over reaction	☐ Sense of identity	☐ Happiness	☐ _______
☐ Silence	☐ Validation	☐ Use of drugs	☐ _______

Please discuss your choices with your therapist or in group.

Please choose if you agree or disagree with statements

When I am in a romantic relationship

		AGREE	DISAGREE
1.	I care only about myself	AGREE	DISAGREE
2.	I feel secure and appreciated	AGREE	DISAGREE
3.	I don't laugh much or feel happy	AGRRE	DISAGREE
4.	I have weekly arguments	AGREE	DISAGREE
5.	I use drugs with my partner	AGREE	DISAGREE
6.	I usually attempt to control and manipulate	AGREE	DISAGREE
7.	I feel pressure to please my partner all the time	AGREE	DISAGREE
8.	I have a lack of privacy	AGREE	DISAGREE
9.	I feel controlled and victimized	AGREE	DISAGREE
10.	I am unable to work or be independent	AGREE	DISAGREE
11.	I have limited access to my family	AGREE	DISAGREE
12.	I don't have too many friendships	AGREE	DISAGREE
13.	I worry about my future	AGREE	DISAGREE
14.	I don't make too many decisions	AGREE	DISAGREE
15.	I lack confidence about my future	AGREE	DISAGREE
16.	I am happy	AGREE	DISAGREE
17.	I respect my partner	AGREE	DISAGREE
18.	I trust my partner	AGREE	DISAGREE
19.	I am loyal to my partner	AGREE	DISAGREE
20.	I have affairs	AGREE	DISAGREE
21.	I don't trust my partner	AGREE	DISAGREE
22.	I hide my drugs and alcohol from my partner	AGREE	DISAGREE
23.	I feel lonely	AGREE	DISAGREE
24.	I am overwhelmed	AGREE	DISAGREE
25.	I break the law and get involved with the legal system	AGREE	DISAGREE

Please discuss your answers with your therapist or in group.

BALANCED LIFE

A balanced life is a life well lived. We seek balance in so many aspects of our lives because we want to feel free of stress, and enjoy the elements of this world with a clear mind set. We must look at our life and fully understand its blue print, purpose and direction. We must assess our goals, plans, and objectives and reflect about how to accomplish them by balancing external (e.g. work, family, friendships, responsibilities) and internal (e.g. health, mind, gratification, self-reward) forces. Happiness is shaped by balance.

We must empower and motivate ourselves in order to be free of conflicts.
Let go of worries and keep feeding joy and harmony in your life.

1. Is your life balanced? YES/NO. Please explain.

____

____

____

____

____

2. How balanced do you feel with your family time? Do you spend enough time with your family? YES/NO. Please explain.

____

____

____

____

____

3. Do you spend enough time by yourself? YES/NO. Please explain.

____

____

____

____

____

4. How do you motivate yourself?

____

____

____

____

____

____

____

5. What must you do to balance your life?

____

____

____

____

____

____

6. What activities must you decrease or increase in order to find balance in your life?
    Please explain.

____

____

____

____

____

7. What can you do in one week to initiate the process of balancing your life?

____

____

____

____

____

8. Are you able to connect with your inner self and enjoy life? YES/NO. Please explain.

____

____

____

____

____

9. Who can help you to find balance in your life?

____

____

____

10. Name at least 5 healthy ways to increase balance in your life.

1.____

2.____

3.____

4.____

5.____

11. How BALANCED is your life today?

Please circle one

0	1	2	3	4	5	6	7	8	9	10
Not balanced					Half balanced					Extremely balanced

Please explain your answer:

____

____

____

____

____

MINDFULNESS IS NOW

Mindfulness is the state of being conscious, completely awake, and fully attentive to the internal and external elements of the present moment. When we are awake from our daily automatic life, we start living what appears to be a surreal dimension of reality. We understand and appreciate the interconnection of everything without judging or falling for life distractions (e.g. politics, sports, organized religion). We have insight and we are insight of the present moment. When we achieve a sublime mindfulness approach to life, we experience great freedom and quality of living. We are no longer conditioned to act and react on auto-pilot. We make wiser choices because we are *awake*. The practice of mindfulness assists us to identify and increase awareness of impulsive, automatically destructive, addictive, risky behaviors.

1. Do you have awareness of your manipulative, destructive, high risky behaviors that may lead you to relapse? YES/NO. Please explain.

____

____

____

____

____

2. Do you decide in an automatic and impulsive way when you decide to use drugs and or alcohol? YES/NO. Please explain.

____

____

____

____

____

3. Are you able to pause, recognize, and challenge emotional and physical experiences that may lead to relapse? YES/NO. Please explain.

____

____

____

____

____

4. Are you able to pause, acknowledge, understand, and be nonjudgmental towards yourself and your experiences? YES/NO. Please explain.

____

____

____

____

5. Are you always conscious of your emotions, reactions and behaviors? YES/NO. Please explain.

____

____

____

____

____

6. What should you do to remain focused and attentive to your recovery?

____

____

____

____

____

7. How much mindful aware are you right NOW?

Please circle one

0	1	2	3	4	5	6	7	8	9	10
Not at all										Extremely

Please explain your answer:

____

____

____

8. Do you find it hard to pay attention to the things you say or do?	YES	NO
9. Have you relapsed because of your impulsive decisions?	YES	NO
10. Do you have difficulty paying attention during tasks?	YES	NO
11. Do you multi-task?	YES	NO
12. Do you act before you think of the consequences?	YES	NO
13. Are you worried about the future or the past?	YES	NO
14. Do you tend to forget daily responsibilities?	YES	NO
15. Do you have difficulty enjoying the present moment?	YES	NO
16. Do you have fun with friends?	YES	NO
17. Are you able to relax?	YES	NO
18. Are you easily distracted by the media?	YES	NO
19. Do you sometimes forget about your recovery?	YES	NO
20. Are you easily influence by others?	YES	NO
21. Have you relapsed in the past due to peer pressure?	YES	NO
22. Do you try to enjoy every moment of the day?	YES	NO
23. Are you attentive to what is happening NOW?	YES	NO

Please reflect, elaborate, and discuss about what your answers are.

____

____

____

____

____

____

____

____

____

____

MAKING DECISIONS

Any decision we make is ultimately our decision. Every day we make wise or poor decisions. Every morning we decide to move on with our daily routine or do something different. Sometimes we decide things without much thinking, and sometimes we pause and think about what will be the best decision. We may move automatically like every other day, or we may reflect about the decision to make. Decision making may be facilitated by emotional, physical, or spiritual experiences, by measuring options and consequences, by perception of pros and cons, by acquiring brainstorming knowledge, by revising and reviewing, by describing and planning, and by values, needs, attitudes, and behaviors.

12. You decided to remain focused on your recovery. What makes this decision **NECESSARY** for you? Please explain your answer.

____

____

____

____

____

13. You decided to pursue your personal goals, desires and dreams with a clear-headed mind, and focus on your recovery. What are the **BENEFITS** of this decision? Please explain your answer.

____

____

____

____

____

14. What was the most difficult decision you have made when you were using drugs or alcohol? What were the **CONSEQUENCES**? Please explain your answer.

____

____

____

____

____

15. What was the most irrational decision you have made when you were using drugs or alcohol? What were the **CONSEQUENCES**? Please explain your answer.

____

____

____

____

____

____

16. Please write seven decisions you made when you were using drugs or alcohol and how they **AFFECTED** your life.

1.____

2.____

3.____

4.____

5.____

6.____

7.____

17. Would you make the same decisions if you were **SOBER**? Please elaborate.

____

____

____

____

____

____

____

18. Please write seven choices you made when you were using drugs or alcohol, which resulted in consequences that you did **NOT EXPECT**. Please explain.

1.____

2.____

3.____

4.____

5.____

6.____

7.____

19. Would you make the same choices if you were **SOBER**? Please explain.

____
____
____
____
____

20. How many times have your **IMPULSIVE** decisions resulted in relapse? Please explain.

____
____
____
____

21. How many times have your **THOUGHTFUL** decisions resulted in relapse? Please explain.

____
____
____
____
____

22. What are the **PROS and CONS** of making a decision after carefully calculating the consequences? Please explain.

____

____

____

____

____

23. *How do you make a choice or a decision?* Write an example of a decision you made today, and explain in detail why and how you came to that decision. Please write the consequences of your decision, pros and cons, and possible alternatives.

____

____

____

____

____

____

____

24. **How capable are you of making WISE and beneficial decisions?**

Please circle one

0	1	2	3	4	5	6	7	8	9	10
Not capable										**Extremely capable**

Please explain your answer.

____

____

____

____

____

____

____

SOLVING PROBLEMS

We will encounter problems during our lives. Sometimes we will have minor problems, and sometimes unthinkable problems. Problems exist, and we are able to resolve them by first identifying symptoms of the problem, seeking information about the problem, brainstorming answers for the problem, choosing the most beneficial resolution for the problem, visualizing and clarifying a plan to resolve the problem, reviewing the proposal to resolve the problem, and putting in action the most positive solution for the problem.

1. When does a **SYMPTOM** of a problem become a problem? (e.g. *symptom-*considering using drugs)

____

____

____

____

2. Are you able to understand symptoms of your personal issues before they become **UNMANAGEABLE** problems? Please write about a problem you had and how you dealt with it.

____

____

____

____

3. Usually, do you **RESOLVE** your problems by yourself, or do you ask for help? Please explain by using an example of a problem you are currently facing.

____

____

____

____

4. Do you **MINIMIZE** your problems? Do you make your problems smaller than they are? YES/NO. Please explain.

____

____

____

____

5. Please list five **PROBLEMS** caused by your addiction.

1. ____

2. ____

3. ____

4. ____

5. ____

6. Please list 4 ways in which you attempted to **CONVINCE** others that you did not have a problem with drugs or alcohol.

1. ____

2. ____

3. ____

4. ____

7. Are you **NOW** aware of the impact of the problems caused by your addiction and how they affected you and the people who care about you? YES/NO. In detail, clarify the impact of the problems caused by your addiction.

____

____

____

____

25. How capable are you in resolving your problems without breaking the law or using drugs?

Please circle one

0	1	2	3	4	5	6	7	8	9	10
Not capable										Extremely

capable

Please explain your answer:

____

____

____

SPIRITUAL JOURNEY

How we view our own existence in the universe is what makes us aware of our actions and reactions to everything. Our physical existence constantly reinvents its time and connects our bodies and souls to the universe. We are the energy that the universe uses to magically and patiently evolve through us. Our bodies are a process that never stands still, and our souls are vessels seeking enlightenment by connecting and feeling the world physically, socially, emotionally, and spiritually.

Our souls constantly animate our bodies and seek balance, harmony, meaning, serenity, purpose, self-actualization, and satisfaction. We are the mindfulness conscience that brings change by letting go of our old limited beliefs. We meditate and seek positive change in our inner selves by embracing our body and soul towards the awakening of compassion, empathy, goodness, and love. We are souls that use bodies. We belong to the multi-level dimensions of the universe.

How do you view your own spiritual existence in the universe?
Please circle one.

0	1	2	3	4	5	6	7	8	9	10
Do not										Extremely

Some Spiritual Principles:

- Honesty
- Acceptance
- Surrender
- Acceptance of Change

- Gratitude
- Forgiveness
- Patience
- Simple living

- Tolerance
- Giving more
- Accepting less
- Living humbly

- Love
- Care
- Compassion
- Self-actualization

1. What do you think gives meaning to your life?

____

____

____

____

____

2. Do you consider yourself spiritual? YES/NO. Please explain.

____

____

____

3. If YES, how important is your spiritual belief? Please explain.

____

____

____

4. Have you ever had a spiritual awakening? YES/NO. Please describe.

____

____

____

5. Do you talk about spirituality or religion with someone? YES/NO. If, yes, who
    and when?

____

____

____

6. Do you believe that spiritual and religious practices enhance the functioning of
    the brain in ways that improve physical and emotional health? YES/NO. Please
    explain.

____

____

____

____

7. Do you think that contemplation about God and other spiritual values awakens
    our conscience and enhances the sensory perceptions about the Self?
    YES/NO. Please explain.

____

____

____

____

8. Think about your body and how it works. Write about a physical illness that you
have experienced and the events that followed.

____

____

____

____

____

9. Do you attend self-help groups such as AA or NA, and practice the 12 Steps of recovery? YES/NO. Please explain.

____

____

____

10. Are you conscious or aware of the impact of your addiction on your body, mind, and soul? YES/NO. Please explain.

____

____

____

11. Are you able to practice mindfulness meditation by putting aside thoughts of the past and future, and staying in the present moment? YES/NO. Please explain.

____

____

____

12. Are you interested in learning more about meditation and relaxation techniques? YES/NO. If you answered yes, explain how beneficial it will be for you to know more about meditation and relaxation techniques.

____

____

____

Discuss with your psychotherapist, ways to obtain information and learn more about meditation and relaxation techniques. You will enjoy a unique self-reflection experience, by cleansing your mind from accumulated thoughts. The mind, soul and body are uniquely designed to be in harmony with each other, and through meditation, we are able to travel into a mindful conscience in a clear, wiser, focused, and profound way.

WORDS AND ACTIONS

Be not afraid of life. Always believe in yourself.

I thought about this statement when shaping many of my thoughts, actions, and attitudes. My inner voice built confidence and assured me that life is worth living. We must appreciate a life of value, confidence, determination, courage, virtue, and understand that fear only exists to be conquered. Fear may become the greatest fertilizer to intensify our personal success.

We can, and we will conquer our fears by BELIEVING and KNOWING ourselves.

BE LIKE WATER

Water does not fight its way but finds a way. If you drop an open bottle of water on the floor, the water will not break the floor. The water will go around and into everything until it finds its destiny in a soft and calm way.

Adjusting to everything is a sublime experience. Accepting first that life is unfair is true awareness. Deciding to become part of your blue print or destiny is genuine understanding of your life purpose. Increasing self-responsibility and self-accountability helps master and acquire self-determination. You are the shape of your thoughts and your actions are the results of such process. The transformation of your shell is called Recovery. Recovery will happen if you choose to let it happen. The choice is yours. No more blaming, no more excuses, no more denial, no more justification, rationalizations, or minimizations. No more fakeness or lies. No more sabotaging your life. Focus on your recovery and apply what you know to be beneficial to you.

WHAT YOU ARE AND WHAT YOU ARE SUPPOSED TO BE

We are what we think, and our thoughts can be believable to us and others. We have a blue print to follow and determine where our life must go. We are to see our lives not as an idea of living, but as a reality to accomplish. Our dreams, plans, and goals have more reasons for us to pursue them, than to let them fade away. We must embrace basic principles and deeply believe in ourselves.

CHANGE

Change is not always wanted, accepted, or respected. We must connect with our emotions in order to understand our actions, and modify our behaviors. We must not ignore our needs to avoid changing our destructive behaviors. We must not forget the execution of forgiveness to avoid change. Change is what connects the universe, and we are part of it. Accept, embrace, and understand that change is a beneficial element in your life.

THE OTHER ONE

We are capable of being at least two characters. We can be the best of us, who is sober and focused on being a productive healthy member of society, or we can be the other one, who lives for addiction and self-destructive careless demons.

Deceit and feigning can deliver intentional means of misinformation, and then, make you relapse. You know when you lie to others and when you lie only to yourself. You know who you are in the presence of others, and who you are when alone. Don't you?

Some of us go through life by interpretation and others by situation. Think of who you are when using drugs and alcohol. Think about who you are when sober and focused on your recovery? Are you the same person? YES/NO.

1. Who are you when under the influence of drugs or alcohol? Are you the self-destructive individual who cares about no one or anything but the subject of addiction and obsession? YES/NO/SOMETIMES. Please explain.

____

____

____

2. Have you robbed when under the influence of drugs or alcohol? YES/NO. Please elaborate.

____

____

____

____

3. Please explain how your personality changes when under the influence of drugs or alcohol? What are you capable of doing when under the influence of substances?

____

____

____

____

4. Did you ever have difficulty remembering events after being under the influence of drugs or alcohol? YES/NO. Please explain.

____

____

____

____

5. Do you want to remain sober and focus on your recovery? YES/NO. Why?

____

____

____

6. What do you need to do to remain the best of **YOU**? That is, sober and focused on being a productive healthy member of society?

____

____

____

7. Explain a past situation that brought out the self-destructive personality?

____

____

____

____

____

____

____

8. Elaborate a possible situation that may bring out the self-destructive personality
   NOW.

   ____

   ____

   ____

   ____

9. How difficult is for you to remain the best of you? (SOBER) Please circle one.

0	1	2	3	4	5	6	7	8	9	10
Not Difficult										**Extremely Difficult**

Please explain your answer.

   ____

   ____

   ____

   ____

10. How many times did you relapse? Please circle one.

0	1	2	3	4	5	6	7	8	9	10	+

Please explain your answer.

   ____

   ____

   ____

   ____

11. How many detoxes have you attended in your life time? Please circle one.

0	1	2	3	4	5	6	7	8	9	10	+

12. When was the last detox you attended? Please elaborate.

   ____

   ____

   ____

   ____

PROS AND CONS OF USING DRUGS AND ALCOHOL

Please write the pros and cons of using drugs and alcohol.

	PROS (e.g. I feel peace)	*CONS* (e.g. I feel sick)
1.		
2.		
3.		
4.		
5.		
6.		
7.		
8.		
9.		
10.		
11.		
12.		

Please reflect, summarize, and discuss the pros and cons.

____

____

____

____

____

____

____

____

____

____

____

WHEN I AM SOBER, I LIKE...

Please complete statements with your behaviors, actions, feelings, attitudes, perceptions, belief system, personality, morals, and other features that you like when sober.

When I am sober, I like ____________________________

When I am sober, I like ____________________________

When I am sober, I like ____________________________

When I am sober, I like ____________________________

When I am sober, I like ____________________________

When I am sober, I like ____________________________

When I am sober, I like ____________________________

When I am sober, I like ____________________________

When I am sober, I like ____________________________

When I am sober, I like ____________________________

When I am sober, I like ____________________________

When I am sober, I like ____________________________

When I am sober, I like ____________________________

When I am sober, I like ____________________________

When I am sober, I like ____________________________

When I am sober, I like ____________________________

When I am sober, I like ____________________________

When I am sober, I like ____________________________

When I am sober, I like ____________________________

When I am sober, I like ____________________________

When I am sober, I like ____________________________

When I am sober, I like ____________________________

When I am sober, I like ____________________________

When I am sober, I like ____________________________

When I am sober, I like ____________________________

When I am sober, I like ____________________________

WHEN I AM SOBER, I ENJOY…

Please complete statements with your behaviors, actions, feelings, attitudes, perceptions, belief system, personality, morals, and other features that you enjoy when sober.

When I am sober, I enjoy____

When I am sober, I enjoy____

When I am sober, I enjoy____

When I am sober, I enjoy____

When I am sober, I enjoy____

When I am sober, I enjoy____

When I am sober, I enjoy____

When I am sober, I enjoy____

When I am sober, I enjoy____

When I am sober, I enjoy____

When I am sober, I enjoy____

When I am sober, I enjoy____

When I am sober, I enjoy____

When I am sober, I enjoy____

When I am sober, I enjoy____

When I am sober, I enjoy____

When I am sober, I enjoy____

When I am sober, I enjoy____

When I am sober, I enjoy____

When I am sober, I enjoy____

When I am sober, I enjoy____

When I am sober, I enjoy____

When I am sober, I enjoy____

When I am sober, I enjoy____

When I am sober, I enjoy____

When I am sober, I enjoy____

When I am sober, I enjoy____

When I am sober, I enjoy____

WHEN I AM SOBER, I KNOW THAT...

Please complete statements with your behaviors, actions, feelings, attitudes, perceptions, belief system, personality, morals, and other elements that you understand and know when you are sober.

When I am sober, I know that _______________________________________

When I am sober, I know that _______________________________________

When I am sober, I know that _______________________________________

When I am sober, I know that _______________________________________

When I am sober, I know that _______________________________________

When I am sober, I know that _______________________________________

When I am sober, I know that _______________________________________

When I am sober, I know that _______________________________________

When I am sober, I know that _______________________________________

When I am sober, I know that _______________________________________

When I am sober, I know that _______________________________________

When I am sober, I know that _______________________________________

When I am sober, I know that _______________________________________

When I am sober, I know that _______________________________________

When I am sober, I know that _______________________________________

When I am sober, I know that _______________________________________

When I am sober, I know that _______________________________________

When I am sober, I know that _______________________________________

When I am sober, I know that _______________________________________

When I am sober, I know that _______________________________________

When I am sober, I know that _______________________________________

When I am sober, I know that _______________________________________

When I am sober, I know that _______________________________________

When I am sober, I know that _______________________________________

When I am sober, I know that _______________________________________

WHEN I USE DRUGS, I....

Please complete statements with your behaviors, actions, feelings, attitudes, perceptions, belief system, personality and morals that affected you when under the influence of drugs.

When I use drugs, I ____

When I use drugs, I ____

When I use drugs, I ____

When I use drugs, I ____

When I use drugs, I ____

When I use drugs, I ____

When I use drugs, I ____

When I use drugs, I ____

When I use drugs, I ____

When I use drugs, I ____

When I use drugs, I ____

When I use drugs, I ____

When I use drugs, I ____

When I use drugs, I ____

When I use drugs, I ____

When I use drugs, I ____

When I use drugs, I ____

When I use drugs, I ____

When I use drugs, I ____

When I use drugs, I ____

When I use drugs, I ____

When I use drugs, I ____

When I use drugs, I ____

When I use drugs, I ____

When I use drugs, I ____

____

WHEN I DRINK ALCOHOL, I...

Please complete statements with your behaviors, actions, feelings, attitudes, perceptions, belief system, personality, and morals that affected you when under the influence of alcohol.

When I drink alcohol, I ____

When I drink alcohol, I ____

When I drink alcohol, I ____

When I drink alcohol, I ____

When I drink alcohol, I ____

When I drink alcohol, I ____

When I drink alcohol, I ____

When I drink alcohol, I ____

When I drink alcohol, I ____

When I drink alcohol, I ____

When I drink alcohol, I ____

When I drink alcohol, I ____

When I drink alcohol, I ____

When I drink alcohol, I ____

When I drink alcohol, I ____

When I drink alcohol, I ____

When I drink alcohol, I ____

When I drink alcohol, I ____

When I drink alcohol, I ____

When I drink alcohol, I ____

When I drink alcohol, I ____

When I drink alcohol, I ____

When I drink alcohol, I ____

When I drink alcohol, I ____

When I drink alcohol, I ____

WHEN I DRINK ALCOHOL AND USE DRUGS, I …

Please complete statements with your behaviors, actions, feelings, attitudes, perceptions, belief system, personality and morals that affected you when under the influence of drugs and alcohol.

When I drink Alcohol and use Drugs, I _______________________________________

When I drink Alcohol and use Drugs, I _______________________________________

When I drink Alcohol and use Drugs, I _______________________________________

When I drink Alcohol and use Drugs, I _______________________________________

When I drink Alcohol and use Drugs, I _______________________________________

When I drink Alcohol and use Drugs, I _______________________________________

When I drink Alcohol and use Drugs, I _______________________________________

When I drink Alcohol and use Drugs, I _______________________________________

When I drink Alcohol and use Drugs, I _______________________________________

When I drink Alcohol and use Drugs, I _______________________________________

When I drink Alcohol and use Drugs, I _______________________________________

When I drink Alcohol and use Drugs, I _______________________________________

When I drink Alcohol and use Drugs, I _______________________________________

When I drink Alcohol and use Drugs, I _______________________________________

When I drink Alcohol and use Drugs, I _______________________________________

When I drink Alcohol and use Drugs, I _______________________________________

When I drink Alcohol and use Drugs, I _______________________________________

When I drink Alcohol and use Drugs, I _______________________________________

When I drink Alcohol and use Drugs, I _______________________________________

When I drink Alcohol and use Drugs, I _______________________________________

When I drink Alcohol and use Drugs, I _______________________________________

When I drink Alcohol and use Drugs, I _______________________________________

When I drink Alcohol and use Drugs, I _______________________________________

When I drink Alcohol and use Drugs, I _______________________________________

When I drink Alcohol and use Drugs, I _______________________________________

When I drink Alcohol and use Drugs, I _______________________________________

GRIEF AND LOSS

Life sometimes brings us unthinkable pain due to grief and loss. We may lose a loved one, a close relationship, a pet, a friend, a job, a lover, our own health, or something or someone we care a lot for. We may feel depressed, anxious, and dreamlike. We may avoid feelings of sadness and despair by taking the path of denial, which may result in substance abuse, mental illness, and health problems. We neglect ourselves and others, and question our ways mentally and spiritually. We may feel lost in the realm wheel of magic, test the boundaries of sanity, and our capacity to remain human.

Loss may change our ways of thinking, and generate emotions and physical reactions that we have never experienced.

Grief is a natural reaction to loss. Grief can take away our sense of belonging to something or someone, and we may feel sad, scared, and lonely. People grieve differently, depending on their life experiences, personality traits, faith, learned coping skills, support system, type of loss, or other factors.

Any loss can cause grief including:

- Death of a loved one
- Loss of a relationship
- Loss of own physical or mental health
- Loss of work or job
- Loss of financial stability
- Loss of possessions or property
- Loss of a loved place or stable home
- Loss of a child moving away
- An injury or disability
- Loss of a friend
- Loss of a lifestyle
- Miscarriage
- Loss of a plan or dream
- Loss of safety
- Loss of faith
- Other_______________________

By grieving we naturally accept loss, and heal by expressing our feelings and utilizing our support system. Do not be afraid to ask for help. Do not limit your tears. You must feel to heal.

We must start the healing process by acknowledging the roots of pain, and conquer the abysm of suffering.

The death of a loved one might encourage you to assess your own feelings about mortality. Grief and loss are personal and we must understand our emotions, seek our support system, and feel the natural process of healing without any resistance or delay.

1. Please reflect on who or what you have lost during your life.

____

____

____

____

____

____

2. Please list the emotions, thoughts and body changes you have had since your loss.

____

____

____

____

____

____

____

3. How has your loss affected your social life?

____

____

____

____

4. How has your loss affected your self-respect?

____

____

____

____

____

5. How has your loss affected your addiction?

____

____

____

____

____

6. How has your loss affected your relationships?

____

____

____

____

____

7. Did you start using drugs or alcohol because of the death of a love one? YES/NO.
Please explain.

____

____

____

____

____

8. Did you relapse in the past or start using drugs to deal with thoughts of loss?
YES/NO. Please explain.

____

____

____

____

____

MY FUTURE BELONGS TO ME

Summarize your plans and goals to maintain your recovery alive and well and meet your needs.

TO IMPROVE THE RELATIONSHIP WITH MYSELF

I will____

____

____

____

TO FIND OR MAINTAIN EMPLOYMENT

I will____

____

____

____

TO FIND OR MAINTAIN HOUSING

I will____

____

____

____

TO PURSUE EDUCATION OR VOCATIONAL SKILLS

I will____

____

____

____

TO HANDLE URGES AND CRAVINGS

I will____

____

____

TO HAVE OR MAINTAIN A MEANS OF TRANSPORTATION

I will____

____

____

TO GAIN OR MAINTAIN A HEALTHY RELATIONSHIP WITH FAMILY

I will____

____

____

TO GAIN OR MAINTAIN A HEALTHY RELATIONSHIP WITH FRIENDS

I will____

____

____

TO LEARN MORE ABOUT MYSELF AND LIFE IN GENERAL

I will____

____

____

TO HAVE FUN AND ENJOY LIFE FREE OF DRUGS AND ALCOHOL

I will____

____

____

TO REGULARLY ATTEND SELF-HELP GROUPS

I will____

____

____

TO GAIN, MAINTAIN, AND EXPAND A HEALTHY SOCIAL NETWORK

I will____

____

____

____

____

TO REDUCE STRESS

I will____

____

____

____

____

TO ELIMINATE CHAOS IN MY LIFE

I will____

____

____

____

TO INCREASE RESPONSIBILITY FOR MY ACTIONS

I will____

____

____

____

TO APPLY PAUSE BEFORE REACTING

I will____

____

____

____

TO RECOGNIZE LAPSES, CRAVINGS AND TRIGGERS FOR RELAPSE

I will____

____

____

____

____

Please add.

TO ____

I will____

____

____

____

____

____

TO ____

I will____

____

____

____

____

TO ____

I will____

____

____

____

____

____

IDENTIFYING MY ISSUES AND BUILDING MY OWN PLANS

	Describe problem symptoms/behaviors/attitudes/addictions/obsessions/compulsions and other matters that you would like to change	How you will resolve/change/improve/eliminate/recover? By doing what? Short Term Goals	Time Frame How long will it take to achieve the Short Term Goals?	How you will resolve/change/improve/eliminate/recover? By doing what? Long Term Goals	Time Frame How long will take to achieve Long Term Goals?
1.					
2.					
3.					
4.					
5.					
6.					
7.					

1. Please elaborate about the benefits of your short and long-term goals, and current achievements.

____

____

____

____

____

____

____

____

____

2. Who can you ask to help you achieve your goals?

____

____

____

____

How CONFIDENT are you in achieving your short and long term goals? Please circle one.

0	**1**	**2**	**3**	**4**	**5**	**6**	**7**	**8**	**9**	**10**
Not Confidence										**Extremely Confidence**

Please explain your answer.

____

____

____

____

SELF-CARE

We care about others and easily forget about ourselves. Self-care is care provided by you to yourself. You need to love and care about your being first before you care about anybody else. You need to identify your beneficial needs and wants, and fulfill your desires and wishes. You need to assure yourself that you are healthy physically, mentally, emotionally, and spiritually.

You need to connect with nature, write a card to a love one, get a massage, meditate in your favorite place, exercise regularly, breath fresh and clean air, listen to music, enjoy a great book, watch a good movie, have fun, spoil yourself with things you can afford, energize yourself with a balanced diet, sleep well, take a nap and rest your body and mind, learn something new, and spend time with true friends who make you laugh.

1. Have you neglected your self-care? YES/NO. Please elaborate.

____

____

____

2. When was the last time you have done something for yourself? Please elaborate.

____

____

____

3. Have you cared for others more and neglected yourself? YES/NO. Please elaborate.

____

____

____

4. How do you think addiction stopped you from caring about yourself?

____

____

____

____

5. What can you do to increase self-care?

____

____

____

____

____

6. Please list the people, things, and places that you care about. Why?

____

____

____

____

____

7. Have you neglected yourself in order to care about others? YES/NO. Please explain.

____

____

____

8. When was the last time you visited your primary doctor? _______________
9. When was the last time you visited your dentist? _______________
10. When was the last time you had a massage? _______________
11. When was the last time you spoiled yourself? _______________
12. When was the last time you laughed and had fun? _______________
13. When was the last time you felt good about yourself? _______________
14. When was the last time you loved being you? _______________
15. When was the last time you smiled at a stranger? _______________
16. When was the last time you were able to relax and feel peace? _______________
17. When was the last time you felt positive about yourself? _______________

18. **How much do you love and care about yourself NOW? Please circle one.**

0   1   2   3   4   5   6   7   8   9   10   +
Do not   **Extremely Love & Care**
Love or Care

Please reflect about your answer.

____

____

____

HEALING WHEN JOURNALING

I encourage you to journal every day. Journaling has a charming effect.

Healing may use reflection and mindful observations by seeking words to describe our goals, strengths, weakness, thoughts, feelings, actions, and attitudes. We may write about our pains, ambitions and dreams, aggressively, patiently or sensitively on paper. Paper takes all types of ink, and any color. We may express our ability to perceive and process our inner selves by constructing awareness of life experiences. We may conclude ideas and re-build self-esteem, self-confidence, and self-determination by reactivating memories and recreating positive and less positive moments. We will teach ourselves by journaling. We may heal, learn, organize, transform, change, create, meditate, recall, imagine, improve, build, re-build, and restore our lives by journaling.

My Journal:

____

____

____

____

____

____

____

____

____

____

____

____

____

____

____

JUST FOR TODAY / DAILY PLANNER
Today is a good day.

Date: _________________________ **Today is:** (circle one)

MONDAY/TUESDAY/WEDNESDAY/THURSDAY/FRIDAY/SATURDAY/SUNDAY

With your daily planner, include if possible, when, with who, where, why and how. Do NOT divert from your daily planning. Always follow your daily goals.

1) ____

2) ____

3) ____

4) ____

5) ____

6) ____

7) ____

What goals did you achieve today? (Circle) **(1) (2) (3) (4) (5) (6) (7)**

- **What would you have done different?** _______________________________

- **Did you follow your daily planner? YES/NO**

- **Did you have any urges or desires to use drugs or alcohol? YES/NO**

- **Were you able to pause before making decisions? YES/NO**

- **Did you apply self-control? YES/NO**

Comments: ____

____

Please rate your day? Please circle one

0	1	2	3	4	5	6	7	8	9	10
Terrible Day										Great Day

Reflect and write about your answers. If possible, discuss your daily planner in groups and with your psychotherapist or sponsor. Make copies of this blank sheet.

MONTHLY PLANNER -MY GOALS

The month of ____ **will be a great month.**

With your monthly planner, include if possible, when, with who, where, why and how. Do NOT divert from your monthly plans. Always follow your monthly goals. Make your goals believable, tangible and possible.

This month I will:

1) ____

2) ____

3) ____

4) ____

5) ____

6) ____

7) ____

8) ____

9) ____

10) ____

11) ____

12) ____

What goals did you achieve? (Circle) **(1) (2) (3) (4) (5) (6) (7) (8) (9) (10) (11) (12)**

- **What would you have done different?** _________________________________

- **Did you follow your Monthly planner? YES/NO**

- **Were you able to pause before making decisions? YES/NO**

- **Did you apply self-control? YES/NO**

Please rate your Month? Please circle one

0	**1**	**2**	**3**	**4**	**5**	**6**	**7**	**8**	**9**	**10**
Terrible Month										Great Month

Reflect and write about your answers. If possible, discuss your monthly planner in groups and with your psychotherapist or sponsor. Make copies of this blank sheet.

CONTRACT

I, ____, agree not to use

drugs or alcohol and remain focused on my recovery.

_______ (initials) I agree to care for myself, to eat well, and to get enough sleep each night.

_______ (initials) I agree to attend self-help groups such as AA/NA at least once a week.

_______ (initials) I agree to use my social support and community resources.

_______ (initials) I agree to make social/family contact with the following individuals:

____

____

____

_______ (initials)

I agree that, if I am having a rough time and come to a point where I may use drugs or

drink alcohol, I will call and make significant contact with any of the following

individuals:

_______________________________ at: #_______________________

_______________________________ at #________________________

_______________________________ at #________________________

Or, if I cannot contact these individuals, I will immediately attend AA/NA group.

_______ (initials) I agree that these conditions are important, and worth following.

_______ (initials) I agree that this is a contract that I am willing to follow. By my word and

honor, I will keep this contract.

Signed_______________________________________Date_______________

Witnessed by_________________________________Date_______________

FEEDBACK

Please send me your suggestions, questions, observations, and comments. I am open to constructive criticism and appreciate your experience and insight. This workbook was designed to support and promote the prevention of relapse by discovering our true selves.

Thank you.

Please contact me at rlima001@gmail.com

How will you rate this workbook? Please circle one

0	1	2	3	4	5	6	7	8	9	10
Terrible										Great

Please elaborate about your choice:

____

____

____

____

____

____

____

Suggestions:

____

____

____

____

____

____

____

____

____

____